Moves for Launching a New Year of Student-Centered Coaching

Moves for Launching a New Year of Student-Centered Coaching

Diane Sweeney

Leanna S. Harris

Julie Steele

FOR INFORMATION:

Corwin

A SAGE Company

2455 Teller Road

Thousand Oaks, California 91320

(800) 233-9936

www.corwin.com

SAGE Publications Ltd.

1 Oliver's Yard

55 City Road

London EC1Y 1SP

United Kingdom

SAGE Publications India Pvt. Ltd.

B 1/I 1 Mohan Cooperative Industrial Area

Mathura Road, New Delhi 110 044

India

SAGE Publications Asia-Pacific Pte. Ltd.

18 Cross Street #10-10/11/12

China Square Central

Singapore 048423

President: Mike Soules

Vice President and
  Editorial Director: Monica Eckman

Acquisitions Editor: Megan Bedell

Content Development
  Editor: Mia Rodriguez

Editorial Assistant: Natalie Delpino

Production Editor: Melanie Birdsall

Typesetter: C&M Digitals (P) Ltd.

Proofreader: Theresa Kay

Cover Designer: Scott Van Atta

Marketing Manager: Melissa Dulcos

Printed in the United States of America

ISBN 9781071890165

Library of Congress Control Number: 2022941015

This book is printed on acid-free paper.

22 23 24 25 26 10 9 8 7 6 5 4 3 2 1

Contents

About the Authors

Diane Sweeney is the author of *The Essential Guide for Student-Centered Coaching* (2020), *Leading Student-Centered Coaching* (2018), *Student-Centered Coaching: The Moves* (2017), and *Student-Centered Coaching From a Distance* (2021), published by Corwin. Each of these books is grounded in the simple but powerful premise that coaching can be designed to more directly impact student learning. Diane spends her time speaking and consulting for schools and educational organizations across the country and abroad. She also designed and is an instructor for a certification program in Student-Centered Coaching from the University of Wisconsin, Madison. When she isn't working in schools, she loves to spend time outside with her family in Denver, Colorado.

Leanna S. Harris is the author of *The Essential Guide for Student-Centered Coaching* (2020), *Student-Centered Coaching: The Moves* (2017), and *Student-Centered Coaching From a Distance* (2021), published by Corwin. She has worked as a teacher and coach and is now a senior consultant with Diane Sweeney Consulting, where she helps schools and districts implement Student-Centered Coaching. Her work is based on the belief that professional development for teachers is most effective when it is grounded in outcomes for student achievement— for every child, every day. Leanna is a passionate skier and cyclist and lives in Denver, Colorado, with her husband and three kids.

Julie Steele has been in public education since 1998 as an elementary teacher, instruction specialist, and consultant. In 2019, she chose to pursue a full-time career in consulting to have a broader impact on students and teachers around the country. Her consulting projects include in-person and online support related to the implementation of Student-Centered Coaching. In addition, Julie has a passion for continuous learning that has led her to present at numerous educational conferences, provide professional learning for school districts around best practices and high-impact instruction, and author several blogs on equity. Julie resides with her husband and kids in the Kansas City, Missouri, area and she spends as much time as she can in her second home in Buena Vista, Colorado.

Introduction

Engaging teachers in coaching is an ongoing process that requires planning and intentionality. Whether you are new to a school or have been there a while, the beginning of the year brings forth the opportunity to envision what our work will look like and the impact it will have on teacher and student learning.

There's nothing like the first few weeks of school; it's a time to reconnect, reimagine, and dream. But just like anything else, starting a new year requires planning and patience. An apt metaphor is the spring gardening season—we just can't wait to plant all those beautiful flowers we picked up at the nursery, but a voice in our head reminds us that before planting, we need to first clean out the beds, till the soil, and add mulch. While this preparation isn't the glamorous part of the job, we know that if we put beautiful plants into soil that isn't ready, they will fail to thrive. The same is true for our coaching: the first few weeks of school are when we do all the work that sets us up for success in the months that will follow.

Starting the year off right always includes establishing a strong principal and coach partnership. We've all recently experienced incredible disruption, and coming together around this work will be an important step forward. That said, this guidebook isn't just about the past few years, but should be viewed as a timeless resource that can be used year after year. We will always need to attend to the important work of practices such as partnering with the principal to get crystal-clear expectations about the coaching role, understanding how to create a culture for coaching, and getting teachers excited to engage. If you are like us, you are ready to plan an amazing new year. Let's craft that plan together.

How to Use This Guidebook

We've designed this guidebook with the goal of providing a clear path for coaches, principals, and district leaders to follow when launching a new year of Student-Centered Coaching. This resource is geared toward returning coaches, those who are new to a school, and those who are new to the role. We've included fifteen coaching moves that will take you through the first four to six weeks of the school year. Think flexibly as you explore these moves. They are meant to be a progression rather than a lockstep list of required actions that every coach must take in the same way. For example, you may already have strong relationships within your school community; if this is the case, you might want to focus on other sections within the guidebook. If you are new to coaching, you may feel the need to follow every move as a road map to implementation. As with everything, where you put your attention will depend on where you are in your journey as a coach.

Throughout the text, we have included strategies, tools, and artifacts to support your work, as well as moments to pause and reflect on your own and with the principal. We truly hope you will mark up these pages with new thinking and ideas to try. We also recommend pairing this guidebook with our other resources, *The Essential Guide for Student-Centered Coaching* (Sweeney & Harris, 2020), *Student-Centered Coaching: The Moves* (Sweeney & Harris, 2016), *Leading Student-Centered Coaching* (Sweeney & Mausbach, 2018), and *Student-Centered Coaching From a Distance* (Sweeney & Harris, 2021). These will take you deeper into the philosophy and practices of Student-Centered Coaching, and they will support your work far beyond the start of the year.

We often find that with coaching, you have to go slow to go fast. Let's slow down and invest carefully in those first few weeks of school so that beautiful things can grow throughout the year.

Note From the Publisher: The authors have provided video and web content throughout the book that is available to you through QR (quick response) codes. To read a QR code, you must have a smartphone or tablet with a camera. We recommend that you download a QR code reader app that is made specifically for your phone or tablet brand.

Resources may also be accessed at **www.dianesweeney.com/launching-tools**

Section I

Build Relationships

Move

1

Be Visible

· ·

Relationships are the foundation for all coaching. Whether you are new to a school, new to the role, or have been in the position for a while, now is the time to be known and visible throughout the school community. This might include helping teachers set up their classrooms, organizing materials, greeting students and families, and supporting the establishment of the day-to-day operation of the school.

In *The Essential Guide for Student-Centered Coaching* (Sweeney & Harris, 2020), we introduced the following figure to compare Student-Centered Coaching with other approaches to instructional coaching. You'll notice that we use the language of *relationship-driven, teacher-centered,* and *Student-Centered Coaching* to describe what we've seen in schools as we've supported coaching over the past decades. This figure describes the role, focus, use of data, and other common coaching behaviors in each type of coaching. We like to think of it as a dartboard. When playing darts, we aim for the bullseye at the center; in this case, the center is student learning. The closer our darts are to the bullseye, the bigger the impact that will be made on teacher and student learning. While it would be nice if we could hit the center every time, we may find ourselves in the outer rings at the start of the school year. This can feel scary because we know that we don't want to get trapped there forever. To avoid this, it's helpful to think of this move as an investment that we make early on with the knowledge that a shift to coaching cycles will soon come.

It's also important to point out that conversations with the principal are an essential step in creating norms and expectations around the coach's duties. We often hear from principals and coaches that anchoring your focus in the following graphic is a concrete way to clarify that while right now a coach may be serving as a resource provider, deeper coaching is right around the corner.

Student-Centered, Teacher-Centered, and Relationship-Driven Coaching

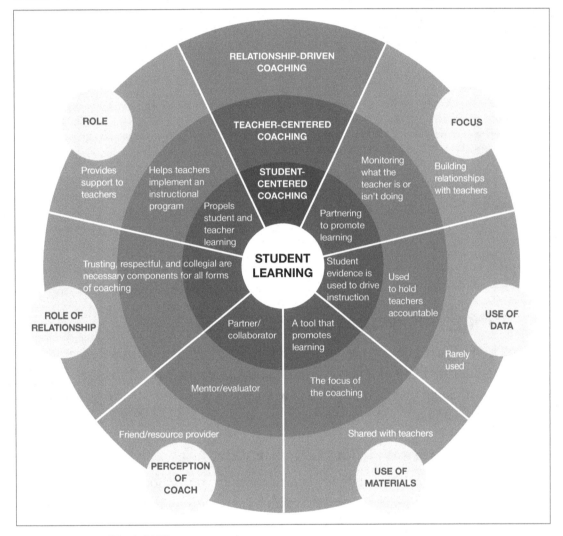

Source: Sweeney and Harris (2020).

Reflect

What does *being visible* mean to you?

_____

_____

_____

_____

_____

_____

_____

_____

_____

What This Move Looks Like

The following strategies are about building relationships and cultivating your identity as a coach. Pretty soon, you won't need to actively work toward being visible because you will have established strong partnerships with teachers.

1. **Create a Welcome Letter or Video**

   Whether you've already been a coach in your school or are just getting started, a welcome letter or video is a great way to introduce yourself, share your beliefs, and build excitement around coaching. Because every year introduces new members of the school community, it's important that this strategy isn't overlooked just because you may have been in the school for a while. Possible audiences for welcome videos include teachers, students, and even families who might be interested in the coaching program. In the Tools and Artifacts section, we share a few examples of welcome letters.

2. **Help Teachers Set Up Classrooms and During Transition Times**

   One of the best times to be out and about in a school is during transition times. Rolling up your sleeves and helping with these kinds of duties sends the message that you are a team player. This includes welcoming students each morning, being present during passing periods, and supervising drop-off and pick-up. Coaches can also help teachers get their learning spaces ready for students. All you need is an informal sign-up sheet, like the example we've provided in the Tools and Artifacts section. Teachers will appreciate all the help they can get as they race to prepare for the arrival of their students.

3. **Help With Beginning-of-the-Year Assessments**

   While we caution against becoming full-time testing coordinators, this doesn't mean we can't help out with assessments at the beginning of the year. When it comes to supporting assessments, we recommend that coaches cover classrooms rather than directly administering the assessments themselves. This reinforces the importance of teachers getting to know their students as learners and protects the coach from becoming an interventionist. Coaches can also support new teachers in understanding how district assessments are administered, where to find necessary resources, and how to input testing data.

4. **Be a Learner**

   One of the most important ways that we can build relationships is by maintaining a learning stance. Being curious and open sends the message that we aren't there to "fix" teachers or tell them what to do. Seek opportunities to spend time in the classroom of an unfamiliar subject, grade level, and so on; doing so reinforces this learning belief because it means a coach recognizes that teachers have something to teach them. Spending time in classrooms as a learner is a great way to make connections with more veteran teachers as well as with those in grade levels you may not have worked with in the past.

How to Partner With the Principal on This Move

It's vital that we work with the principal to create boundaries around these early-in-the-year tasks or we run the risk that they will become our core work. We recommend the coach and principal talk through the following questions to ensure that they are set up to shift to coaching cycles as the school year gets up and running.

- What are some early-in-the-year tasks that the coach can help teachers with?

- What is the start date for kicking off coaching cycles?

- How will we monitor the tasks the coach is involved in?

Moving Forward

As you plan to be visible in the first few weeks of school, think broadly about the school community. Get to know, or continue to build relationships with, the principal, teachers, specialized teachers (art, music, and PE), and even parents. The goal is for everyone to not only know you but also to understand the role of the coach. This investment will pay off as the school year shifts into high gear.

Next Steps

How will you foster relationships by being visible in the first few weeks of school?

_____

_____

_____

_____

_____

_____

_____

_____

_____

_____

_____

_____

_____

_____

_____

_____

_____

_____

Tools and Artifacts

VIDEO

Student-Centered
Coaching in the First
Few Weeks of School

SAMPLE

Sign-Up Sheet for
Informal Support

SAMPLE

Welcome Letters

www.dianesweeney.com/launching-tools

To read a QR code, you must have a smartphone or tablet with a camera. We recommend that you download a QR code reader app that is made specifically for your phone or tablet brand.

Move 2

Join PLCs or Grade-Level or Department Meetings

Most schools have established collaborative time through professional learning communities (PLCs), grade-level meetings, or department meetings. These are opportunities for coaches to make connections with a wide array of teachers. The key is to remember that at this point in the year, the focus must be on building relationships rather than assigning tasks or directing conversations.

How coaches engage in team meetings will depend on how long they have been in the school. If you are new to a school, you may be about meeting as many teachers as possible. If you have been coaching at the school for a while, you may wish to focus on reconnecting. In either scenario, teachers are often protective of their meeting time, so it's helpful to think of yourself as a guest rather than as a facilitator at this stage of the process. As the year progresses, there will probably be opportunities to support through facilitation; for now, it's okay to just listen.

Reflect

What does *joining team meetings* mean to you?

_____

_____

_____

_____

_____

_____

_____

_____

_____

_____

What This Move Looks Like

This move is as much about holding back as it is about jumping in. It's amazing how much we can hear when we dial back our inclination to solve problems for people and instead try to understand where they are coming from. Following are some ways you can engage while still maintaining a light touch.

1. **Keep an Open Mind**

   When it comes to working with teachers, wondering is more powerful than knowing. This means we must avoid making assumptions about individuals and teams. We can't underestimate the complexity of teaching; keeping this in mind is imperative if we hope to build trusting relationships. Entering each and every conversation with an open mind is how we model a learning stance.

2. **Avoid Taking Over**

   It can be tempting to take over collaborative conversations and shut down the voices of others, especially when a group is demonstrating confusion, cognitive dissonance, or frustration. We want to right the ship and keep things moving, so we jump in and take control.

This is particularly damaging during the relationship-building stage of the school year; we'd hate to have teachers walk away from a conversation thinking that we have an agenda or that we think we know better. As the year progresses, the coach's role during these meetings may shift to a more facilitative one, but for now, our purpose is to build relationships.

3. **Listen and Self-Monitor**

A meeting is a great time to practice strategies for listening, self-monitoring, note taking, and positive body language. Think of it as a chance to cheer teachers on, listen for openings for future coaching, and understand where teachers are coming from as the year begins. Achieving this depends on being an effective listener. We can enhance and refine our listening skills by self-monitoring the following behaviors:

Behaviors That Take Us Away From Effective Listening

- Interrupting the speaker
- Providing advice too quickly
- Thinking about our response when the speaker is still speaking
- Being uncomfortable with silence
- Piggybacking or hijacking the conversation
- Bringing our own agenda to the conversation

Source: Sweeney and Harris (2020).

4. **Explore Unfamiliar Curriculum With Teachers**

Whenever teachers encounter new curricula or content, a coach can be a thinking partner for exploring and making sense of how to move forward. Rather than thinking about this as a training or professional development session, think of it as a time to review, explore, and understand a new resource. Such an approach will lead to openings for future coaching, as it sends a strong message that the coach is a partner, rather than someone who is there to hold teachers accountable for implementing curricular resources with fidelity. Some guiding questions for curriculum review include:

◗ How is the new curriculum organized?

◗ How does the learning progress across any given unit or chapter?

◗ What are some considerations around pacing when it comes to the new materials?

◗ As we review the resource, what questions or concerns come to mind?

5. **Include This Move on Your Sign-Up for Informal Coaching**

We can't wait for an engraved invitation to join team collaboration; we have to take action to create opportunities for this to happen. Maybe teachers don't think to invite a coach, or maybe they don't trust that a coach is there to support them in a respectful and responsive way. This may be due to what coaching has looked like in the past, how well teachers know the coach, or other factors. Creating the opportunity to join team conversations may come down to putting this option on a sign-up sheet that you share with teachers early in the year.

How to Partner With the Principal on This Move

Principals often view the first few days of the school year as a time to get teachers up to speed around expectations. Yet it can be damaging when this responsibility lands on the shoulders of coaches. To get on the same page, a principal and coach can work through the following questions to ensure that this move is used in a way that builds trusting relationships with teachers and doesn't eliminate opportunities for deeper coaching as the year progresses.

◗ What message will we send to teachers about why a coach will be joining team collaboration?

◗ Which teams will the coach focus on, and why?

◗ Will the principal also join team collaboration time? If so, will the purpose be the same or different?

Moving Forward

We know that relationships are the foundation for coaching. But it's important to keep in mind that how we join team meetings at the beginning of the year will change quite a lot as the year progresses. The coach as facilitator, guide, and co-planner will become essential elements of Student-Centered Coaching. But for now, it's okay to join as a thinking partner, listener, and friend.

Next Steps

How will you tap into existing team meetings to build relationships?

_____

_____

_____

_____

_____

_____

_____

_____

_____

_____

_____

_____

_____

_____

_____

_____

_____

_____

_____

_____

_____

_____

_____

_____

_____

_____

_____

Tools and Artifacts

TOOL

Self-Assessment:
How Am I as a
Listener?

PODCAST

Student-Centered
Coaching: The Podcast,
Episode 7, With
Joy Casey

TOOL

Language for
Exploring a
Resource or
Curriculum

www.dianesweeney.com/launching-tools

Move

3

Offer Mentoring Support to New Teachers

· ·

While we recognize that there are differences between mentoring and Student-Centered Coaching, that doesn't mean that a coach can't provide differentiated support to teachers who are new to the profession, school, or district. Not only does this help new teachers get their feet under them, it's a great way to build relationships for future coaching.

We often encounter districts where mentoring sits on the coaches' plates. In other places, there are dedicated mentors who are staffed at the district level. Also common are districts that assign mentoring to fellow classroom teachers. We'd argue that no matter how mentoring is designed, there can never be too much support provided to new teachers, especially when many are coming through pathways of alternative certification due to teacher shortages. Working with new teachers in these first few weeks is an opportunity for connection and collaboration right out of the gate.

Reflect

How do you envision providing mentoring support to new teachers?

_____

_____

_____

_____

_____

_____

_____

_____

_____

_____

_____

What This Move Looks Like

Signaling to new teachers that you are there for them is an important first step. From there, you can use the following strategies to help them start the year strong.

1. **Don't Expect Coaching Cycles Right Away**

   This part of the year is about setting ourselves up for future coaching. We need to be sensitive to the fact that some newer teachers may not have the bandwidth to engage in full coaching cycles for a while. They may be overwhelmed with learning about the curricular resources, methods of delivering instruction, and the social and emotional needs of their students (and themselves). While we hope that new teachers will participate in coaching cycles later in the school year, it can be a relief to them to acknowledge that they may not be ready right away. So, let's not force new teachers into coaching cycles. Rather, we can provide informal support and messages that there will be opportunities to engage on a deeper level as the year progresses.

2. **Work With New Teachers to Develop Their Identities and Belief Systems**

If we hope to create schools where teachers thrive over the long term, then we need to guide them to establish a clear vision around their identities and belief systems. In other words, we need teachers to feel activated so they'll dig into the complex and challenging work that lies before them. One way a coach can do this is by engaging new teachers in conversations about why they became an educator and what they need in order to feel happy and empowered. Taking this step means a coach might need to slow down and create space for these conversations, even though they aren't about the curriculum, assessments, or pacing guides. What a great way to cultivate strong relationships right from the start! The following coaching questions give you some ideas about how you might have these conversations. We find that they are beneficial either individually or with small groups of new teachers.

Questions for Coaching Into Identity and Belief Systems

- Why did you decide to become an educator?
- What was your experience as a student?
- If you could change the world, what would that look like?
- What worries you most about being a teacher?
- Fill in the blank: *I am most fulfilled when ___.*

3. **Explore the Curriculum and Materials With New Teachers**

Creating a culture that focuses on student learning begins on day one. When we were new teachers, we thought about the curriculum as being something to be *followed* rather than something to be *understood*. This usually translated to being handed a resource with the instructions to let the coach know if you had any questions. This process doesn't build teacher clarity because it isn't reflective. An alternative approach would be to work with new teachers to develop their understanding of how the curriculum progresses, what the learning targets are (or might be), and how to formatively assess along the way.

4. **Create a New Teacher Cohort**

Most teachers find that they bond very quickly with other new teachers. This is a starting point for welcoming them into the school community. Coaches can facilitate this by creating a cohort for new teachers to engage in needs-based professional learning. This may take place over the lunch hour, after school, or during team time. We like to think of this as a sacred space where new teachers can build their own sense of efficacy by studying, sharing, and exploring whatever they might need, including strategies for communicating with parents, ideas around classroom management, work on identity and beliefs, ways to engage students as learners, and learning around a program or curriculum.

How to Partner With the Principal on This Move

It can be tempting for principals to assign new teachers to a coaching cycle right out of the gate. As we explained earlier, this may be a less productive strategy than supporting new teachers informally until they are ready to dive into a full coaching cycle. Following are some questions a coach and principal can discuss as they think about how they might encourage reflection and community among new teachers.

▶ What is our best first step for supporting new teachers?

▶ When can we find time for a learning cohort for new teachers?

▶ How will the principal introduce the coach to new teachers, and what will the message be about how new teachers will be expected to engage in coaching?

Moving Forward

We can't expect new teachers to last if we don't support them. We also don't have to think of mentoring and coaching as two different things. Wrapping support around our newest teachers at the beginning of the year sends a strong signal that they are learners within the broader school community. As we move through the year, the support that is provided will extend and grow deeper. This is just the beginning of both coaching and a trusting relationship.

Next Steps

How will you provide mentoring support to new teachers?

_____

_____

_____

_____

_____

_____

_____

_____

_____

_____

_____

_____

_____

_____

_____

_____

_____

_____

_____

_____

_____

_____

_____

_____

_____

_____

_____

Tools and Artifacts

VIDEO

Student-Centered
Mentoring

BLOG

Three Strategies for Helping
New Teachers Develop
Successful Lessons by
Amanda Brueggeman

TOOL

Survey for
New Teachers

www.dianesweeney.com/launching-tools

Move 4

Support Teachers to Build Classroom Community

· ·

There is so much to do in the first few weeks of school. Teachers will be reconnecting with their students and setting up classrooms, and many will be learning about new curricula and programs. While we may feel compelled to jump right into content on the first day of school, we can't overlook the importance of building community in the classroom; if we don't make time for this, we set ourselves up for challenges related to student behavior and engagement as the year progresses. We simply can't risk setting up a school year where weak teacher and student relationships lead to ongoing behavior challenges in classrooms.

Reflect

Why is it important to coach into building classroom community?

_____

_____

_____

_____

_____

_____

_____

_____

_____

_____

What This Move Looks Like

As coaches, we can support teachers as they work to build relationships with their students. We can accomplish this using the following strategies.

1. **Work With Teachers to Create a Sense of Belonging Among Students**

   Coaching into building relationships with students can feel like a no-go zone for coaches because it sometimes feels sensitive and, in some ways, private. Yet we know that relationships are the most important factor when it comes to both classroom management and student learning. For this reason, we have to learn how to go there, especially at the beginning of the year. If we learn how to ask questions around relationship building while maintaining positive intent, we set ourselves up to nurture both our relationships with teachers and their relationships with students. The following questions can be built into check-ins with teachers who are focused on (or concerned about) classroom management.

Language That Creates a Sense of Belonging Among Students

- When you envision your classroom community, what do you hope it will feel like for each of your students?

- What specific steps will you take to engage students who haven't felt a sense of belonging in school?

- If school is held virtually or on a hybrid schedule, how will you build community so that all students feel connected?

- How will each student's voice be invited, honored, and valued by you and fellow students?

- What norms will be created and monitored to ensure that the students' voices are heard and honored?

- What routines will you create to allow all students to participate in the classroom community?

- As the coach, how can I support you in creating this community with your students?

Source: Sweeney and Harris (2021).

2. **Work With Teachers to Establish Rituals and Routines**

The act of setting classroom expectations through the use of rituals and routines is a necessary strategy for creating a productive classroom. When students don't have a clear idea of what's expected or how they fit into the classroom environment, they may disengage or disrupt the learning.

Working with teachers to break down a lesson into its most basic components creates the opportunity to think through routines for learning. For example, during a co-planning session, a coach may ask the teacher how students will transition throughout the lesson, or maybe about the steps that will be provided to students regarding classroom materials. Some guiding questions may include:

▶ What rituals and routines will you create to allow all students the opportunity to participate in the classroom community?

▶ What norms will be created and monitored to ensure the students' voices are heard and honored?

▶ How will we intervene if rituals and routines aren't being honored by students?

3. **Find Ways to Support Teachers When Community Breaks Down**

Things may become delicate if we encounter situations where breakdowns caused by issues related to the classroom community are occurring. These situations may lead a principal to try to solve the problem by directing a teacher to work with the coach on classroom management. We'd argue that this isn't a productive way to build trust in the coaching program. If the principal would like to nudge a teacher to work with a coach to address these issues, it can be helpful to frame the message as follows: "We are aiming to start the school year with strong relationships with our students, and your coach could be a good resource on this." While the difference between these approaches may seem nuanced, the second example is all about providing a learning-focused rationale for the recommendation rather than simply directing a teacher to a coach because the principal said so. (We'll explore more ways your principal can advocate for coaching later in this guidebook.)

Another way these issues can be addressed is to be proactive in forging conversations around them right from the start. Coaches might take the following steps to initiate these conversations:

▶ Send an email to teachers letting them know that you would like to be a thinking partner as they plan how they will build their classroom community.

▶ Create a cohort of teachers who would like to explore this as a group.

▶ Develop professional learning on this topic.

How to Partner With the Principal on This Move

Just as with anything, the more a coach and principal are on the same page, the clearer things will become. We often carry our own ideas about how to best support things like engagement and classroom management. Following are some questions to ask each other to ensure that there is clarity of purpose:

▶ Where are opportunities to discuss strategies for building relationships with students in the first few weeks of school?

▶ How will these conversations connect with school initiatives or resources that focus on this topic?

▶ How will the school leadership connect with students who are struggling to engage now and as the school year progresses?

Moving Forward

As we work to build community, an important role for coaches is to help teachers create belonging and access for all students. Partnering with teachers and the principal will support our students to thrive in ways that go far beyond the lesson of the day.

Next Steps

How will you support teachers to build a strong classroom community in the first few weeks of school?

_____

_____

_____

_____

_____

_____

_____

_____

_____

_____

_____

_____

_____

_____

_____

_____

_____

_____

_____

Tools and Artifacts

BLOG

How Can I Help Teachers
Build Community in
the Classroom?

TOOL

Coaching to Support
Classroom Community

VIDEO

How Do We Engage
Students in Building
Community?

www.dianesweeney.com/launching-tools

Section II

Make Intentional Decisions With the Principal

Move

5

Establish How You'll Work as a Principal and Coach Team

It's the principal's role to go beyond simply supporting a coaching effort to actually leading it. Strong leaders build partnerships with the coach, understand how to separate coaching from evaluation, and position the coach to be a valued resource within the school community. Yet many leaders receive very little direction regarding how to best deploy a coach.

To make things even trickier, principals are asked to wear an increasingly growing number of hats. Principals are often pulled from one crisis to another, which makes it easy to understand the temptation to use the coach as a quasi-administrator. But utilizing coaches to manage discipline issues, administer testing, and lead administrative tasks is a good way to confuse teachers about the coaching role. While we understand the temptation to use coaches to help with administrative duties, we know that the most meaningful coaching happens when there is a strong partnership in which the coach can focus on work that directly impacts teacher and student learning. Therefore, it's important to set up this partnership early in the year. Taking this step will get the coaching effort off to a solid start.

Reflect

Why do you think it's important to have a strong relationship with your school leadership?

_____

_____

_____

_____

_____

_____

_____

_____

_____

What This Move Looks Like

As we mentioned, having a strong principal and coach partnership will make or break a successful coaching initiative. Below are some strategies to build these partnerships right from the beginning.

1. **Set Norms for Working Together**

   Even if you've worked with your principal in the past, either as a teacher or as a coach, it's important to establish or reestablish norms for working together at the beginning of each school year. This involves having a discussion about when you'll meet, what each of your roles will be, and how you'll communicate about the coaching work that is taking place. Assuming a mindset of "we know each other really well, so it will all just work out" instead of intentionally addressing these topics can lead to a lack of direction and differing expectations. Even with the best intentions, it's hard to have a true partnership when both parties aren't on the same page.

2. **Plan for When and How You'll Meet**

Without a commitment to meet regularly, it's easy to see how weeks and even months can go by with only on-the-fly communication between a principal and coach. Therefore, we suggest planning to meet weekly, and that this time is scheduled on the calendar to happen on a specific day and time. In addition to committing the time to collaborate, it's also critical to establish what you will be discussing in these meetings. It's all about setting a clear expectation that the discussion will focus on the current work the coach is engaging in, trends that are being seen by the principal, and the next steps for ongoing professional learning. In doing so, you will avoid getting stuck in the rut of talking about, and being tasked with, everything under the sun *besides* coaching. In the Tools and Artifacts section, we include an example of an agenda for meetings that aligns with this process.

3. **Define Both of Your Roles**

There may be nothing more important to set a coach up for success than making sure that their role is clearly defined. This keeps coaches from taking on an evaluative role, being seen as part of the administrative team, or being pulled to take on countless other duties that have little to do with impacting learning. Clarifying the coaching role also helps when it comes to communicating about coaching to the broader school community.

In addition to defining the coach's role, it's valuable to understand the principal's role in leading the coaching effort. This helps both members of the partnership to hold one another accountable, support each other, and each stay in their appropriate lane. The following figure from *Leading Student-Centered Coaching* (Sweeney & Mausbach, 2018) offers suggestions for how coaches and principals might start thinking about each of their roles.

Behaviors of School Leader and Coach in Providing Pressure and Support

SCHOOL LEADER	COACH
Sets high expectations for teacher and student learning	Provides support to teachers so they can meet the expectations that have been established by the school leadership
Holds teachers accountable for meeting the needs of the students	Organizes coaching so that it aligns with the accountability measures that are in place
Establishes a vision and sets priorities for how to move student learning forward	Prioritizes work that has the most potential to impact student learning
Makes strategic use of the coach to move teacher learning forward	Articulates the role of the coach and engages teachers in the coaching process
Leads the decision making about the scope and breadth of the content that is taught	Helps teachers design instruction that aligns with expectations about the content that is taught
Knows what high-quality instruction looks like and sets the expectation that this is the norm throughout the school	Skillfully supports teachers to implement high-quality instruction
Is aware of situations when students are underperforming and works to address the issue	Works with teachers across all levels of performance
Leads data-driven conversations with teachers and the coach	Participates in data-driven conversations with teachers and the principal
Spends time in classrooms and provides teachers with feedback as a result of the observations	Spends time in classrooms to support the delivery of effective instruction
Creates the structure and time for teachers to collaborate with each other and the coach	Designs and facilitates collaboration among teachers

Source: Sweeney and Mausbach (2018).

4. **Get Clear on Confidentiality**

When we first started coaching many years ago, our motto was "confidentiality is king." We now know that, while well-intentioned, keeping our coaching work a secret in order to protect teachers actually undermines the open, risk-taking, learner-centered culture that is needed for coaching to thrive. By taking the time to clarify what is meant by *transparency* and how coaching will be discussed, a principal and coach are able to forge a partnership in which coaching and ongoing learning are both expected and celebrated.

Can—Do vs. deficit—just like w/the kids

So, rather than focusing on confidentiality, we take the stance of protecting the respect and dignity of teachers by taking an asset-based perspective. This ensures that a principal and coach can openly discuss their work while honoring the learning of others. In the Tools and Artifacts section, you'll find an example of norms for sharing our coaching work.

How to Partner With the Principal on This Move

This move is all about partnering with the principal. As you think about each of the ideas we've shared, consider some additional questions to guide the conversations that you will be having together.

> ▸ What is your vision for coaching, and how does it translate into your expectations for the role?

> ▸ How can we be sure to separate coaching from supervision and evaluation?

> ▸ How can we talk about the coaching work in a way that's professional, transparent, and asset based?

> ▸ What are the best ways to support each other so everyone in our school can get the most benefit from coaching?

> ▸ If there is more than one coach in a school, or a coach is part-time, how will we collaborate?

Moving Forward

Coaching is hard, messy work. While it may feel good to have the trust of a school administrator to "do your thing," this kind of hands-off approach is not enough to ensure that coaching will really thrive. Instead, principal-and-coach teams need to start the year off right by making sure that all the pieces are in place for a strong partnership. In this way, coaching can truly reach its maximum potential.

Next Steps

How will you work to establish a strong principal and coach team at the beginning of the year?

How can I clarify/define the role so that people feel/see the value? Gretchen - very rigid so I had to tread lightly - how to find the middle ground?

Tools and Artifacts

TOOL

Principal and
Coach Agreement

SAMPLE

Agenda for Principal
and Coach Meetings

TOOL

Norms for Sharing
Our Coaching Work

www.dianesweeney.com/launching-tools

Move 6

Decide How You Will Organize Your Coaching Schedule

As we've mentioned, it's important to spend the first few weeks of school building relationships and giving teachers space to establish their classroom communities. But that doesn't mean we can't also begin thinking about how we'll organize ourselves so we can shift into deeper and more structured coaching work in the coming weeks.

Carefully planning how we will build a schedule ensures that we don't get pulled in a million different directions, ending up with no time to engage in coaching cycles. Rather, when we organize our schedule to maximize time for coaching, it will be crystal clear that this is how our time is meant to be spent.

Reflect

As you think about this school year, what's your vision for your coaching schedule?

_____

_____

_____

_____

_____

_____

_____

_____

_____

_____

What This Move Looks Like

Having a schedule that allows time for coaching cycles will set you up for success. Following are some things to take into consideration as you prepare to move into more structured coaching work.

1. **Align Coaching Cycle Rounds to the Flow of the School Year**

   The Essential Guide for Student-Centered Coaching (Sweeney & Harris, 2020) introduced the idea of scheduling coaching cycles using a system of rounds. This can be helpful because no matter the school or district, there are some predictable elements to the flow of the year. The following figure provides a step-by-step guide and an example of coaching cycle rounds. You'll notice that we've accounted for the first weeks being filled with getting to know kids and setting up routines. Winter holidays, spring break, and other days off are sprinkled throughout the calendar. Testing takes up a few weeks in the spring, and maybe at other times as well. As you look for opportunities in your own school calendar, be mindful of the fact that your role may shift based on these factors. Don't worry;

instead, you can recognize the natural flow of the school year and plan for four-to-six-week rounds for cycles around those particular times.

Launching Coaching Cycles

1. Decide when the rounds for coaching cycles will occur. Align with the curriculum calendar if possible.

2. Before each round, invite teachers to participate. They can choose who they will include in the cycle.

3. Build a schedule based on who is in the next round.

4. At the end of the round, engage in end-of-cycle reflections.

5. Launch a new round.

Example of Coaching Cycle Rounds

1. October to early November

2. Mid-November to early December

3. January to mid-February

4. March to mid-April

2. **Plan for a Balance of Formal and Informal Coaching**

While we strongly believe that the biggest impact on teacher and student learning comes from engaging in coaching cycles, we also recognize that there are other things that coaches need to be doing with their time. This includes co-planning single lessons or units, providing resources for teachers, attending PLCs, district training, and regular meetings with your school principal, and perhaps planning for and delivering schoolwide professional development.

We recommend that as soon as the school year is up and running, coaches strive to be in full or mini coaching cycles for 60 percent of their time, leaving the other 40 percent for everything else. Now is a good opportunity to think about what is on your plate and whether it will ultimately allow for this 60/40 balance in your schedule, as is represented in the following figure.

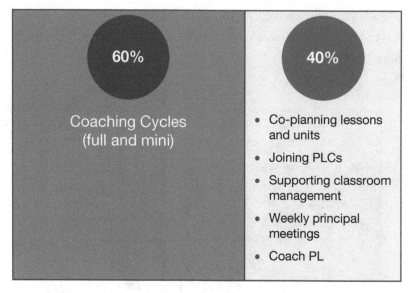

www.dianesweeney.com

3. **Be Deliberate When Scheduling for Dual Roles or in More Than One School**

Dedicating 60 percent of your time to coaching cycles can be challenging for a full-time coach at a single school. This becomes even more tricky when we coach half-time or share our time between two schools. We have seen many coaches try a variety of creative scheduling formulas in these situations, and there are a few elements that they have in common:

▶ **Flexibility**—Work with school or district leaders to build a schedule that can "flip" every quarter or semester instead of being locked into the same setup for the entire year.

▶ **Balance**—Think in terms of "heavy" and "light" touch with teachers. You may only be in cycles with one teacher at a time, but you can still do lots of meaningful informal coaching with others.

▶ **Creativity**—Use shared documents and virtual platforms to communicate so you don't always have to be in the same place at the same time.

4. **Make Your Schedule Public**

We often hear coaches lamenting that teachers don't understand how Student-Centered Coaching works or don't know what coaches actually do all day long. To clarify your role and celebrate coaching, make sure your schedule is visible to everyone. As you begin each new round of coaching cycles, publish your schedule in a newsletter or email to staff and post it on the door of your office. Even if you aren't yet to the place of being in rounds, you can put out a weekly schedule instead. Taking this step makes it clear what you do as a coach, who you work with, and the value of coaching.

How to Partner With the Principal on This Move

Since the principal typically guides the master schedule, it's important to make sure that you have the ability to function successfully within that schedule. When thinking about how to organize your coaching schedule, consider the following questions to discuss together.

- ▶ How can the master schedule be organized to maximize time for coaching and collaboration?

- ▶ When are the optimal times for coaching cycle rounds? What times of the year are less optimal for cycles?

- ▶ What are all the things the coach is expected to do at the school? How can we protect the coach's time so they can spend the majority in coaching cycles?

- ▶ How can we organize the schedule so we can maximize the coach's time in more than one school or a dual role?

Moving Forward

For some of us, thinking about setting up a schedule can feel overly formal and forced. We may feel more comfortable just letting things evolve naturally. While this approach may work for some, we often find that it prohibits us from moving into deeper and more impactful coaching work. For this reason, it's important to be intentional about scheduling—across the school year and in our day-to-day work. This helps us define our role and ensures that we have the time and space to engage in meaningful coaching.

Next Steps

How will you be strategic in organizing your schedule to get the most out of coaching?

_____

_____

_____

_____

_____

_____

_____

_____

_____

_____

_____

_____

_____

_____

_____

_____

_____

_____

_____

_____

_____

_____

_____

_____

Tools and Artifacts

BLOG

Student-Centered
Coaching Cycles

SAMPLE

Coaching
Schedules

TOOL

Options for Scheduling
When Sharing Schools

www.dianesweeney.com/launching-tools

Move 7

Be Thoughtful About Who You Will Engage With First

··

In many schools and districts, coaching is seen as a tool to "fix" struggling teachers. Principals assign certain teachers to work with the coach, and being coached is often something done out of compliance rather than authentic engagement. To shift this approach, principals and coaches have to create a culture in which everyone sees themselves as a learner who has the potential to continue to grow professionally. Setting the tone that working with a coach is both a privilege and responsibility is key to our success.

That said, if we simply leave participation to chance, we may find that the coach is only able to work with a few highly engaged teachers. Therefore, we need to be thoughtful about who we start with and create systems in which teachers feel comfortable and motivated to work with us.

Reflect

How do you decide who to engage first as you move into deeper coaching?

_____

_____

_____

_____

_____

_____

_____

_____

_____

_____

_____

What This Move Looks Like

By the time you're ready to start the first round of coaching cycles, you have likely spent time working to build strong relationships with teachers. Hopefully, this results in your feeling ready to consider who might be the best candidates for your first round of coaching cycles.

1. **Work With the Principal to Create an "All-In" Culture**

   It's our job to make sure that coaching feels relevant and welcoming to all teachers. To do this, we need to work with the principal to plan how we will engage teachers based on a variety of factors, as described in the following graphic. For example, teachers who are new to teaching and/or new to the school may not yet be embedded in collaborative processes like coaching cycles and PLCs. The strategies for engaging this group might include building rapport, providing mentoring, and working together on the curriculum. Teachers who are new to teaching and are already collaborating might be ready for a coaching cycle earlier, and teachers who are not actively collaborating might be willing to lead the learning of others. Lastly, experienced teachers who are highly collaborative are probably already engaged. The key is to avoid having a roster that is dominated by just one of these groups, as it will create the perception that coaching is only for a certain slice of the teaching population. Seeking balance across all four quadrants means we have to be thoughtful about how we engage different teachers with different needs.

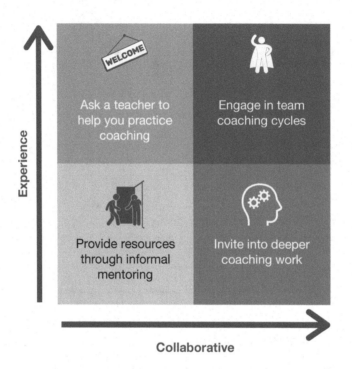

2. **Look to Teacher Leaders for Building Energy**

As we think about teachers who sit in the two quadrants on the right side of the graphic above, we may be thinking of some of the teacher leaders in our school. This may refer to department or grade-level heads, members of building leadership teams, or those who lead even without an official designation. Tapping into this group early on is a great way to build energy around the coaching effort since teacher leaders are often the same ones who are naturally collaborative. We also feel that it's a reasonable expectation for a principal to encourage these folks to step up and be role models for others as part of their leadership positions. More ideas will be shared for engaging teacher leaders later in this guidebook.

3. **Avoid Coaching Only New or Struggling Teachers**

We all know the adage that "a picture is worth a thousand words." Similarly, our coaching roster speaks volumes about our beliefs about coaching. While it may feel tempting (and even essential) to start the year with only new and struggling teachers, consider the wider message delivered by such an approach. We want everyone to understand and embrace the idea that "coaching is for everyone," and who we work with should reflect that very belief. The bottom line is that we want to have a well-rounded roster as we move into deeper coaching.

4. **Ask a Teacher to Help You Practice Your Coaching**

   Perhaps the easiest way to ensure you get off to a good start is to invite a teacher to help you practice in a coaching cycle. Think of someone you already have a strong relationship with, or perhaps someone you taught with before becoming a coach. By inviting someone to help you in this way, you are showing yourself to also be a learner, not the "resident expert" that coaches have often been portrayed to be. In addition, you are setting yourself up for a successful experience you can then use to gain momentum for future coaching work.

How to Partner With the Principal on This Move

As you can see from the previous section, there is a lot here that involves collaboration with the principal. Creating a culture in which coaching can thrive is very much driven by the school leader. As a coach, here are a few questions you can use with your principal to guide the partnership toward being successful with this move.

▶ What is your vision for our school culture? How can we best communicate this with teachers?

▶ What does authentic engagement in coaching look like?

▶ What are some additional ways to support our new teachers so there is time to coach more experienced teachers as well?

Moving Forward

After investing time in building relationships with teachers, it can feel nerve-wracking to think about moving into more formal coaching work. *What if no one signs up?* is the question that weighs on the minds of many coaches at the beginning of each school year. Sure, your time could be filled up pretty quickly if your principal required that every new teacher start the year by working with you, but we encourage you to take the long view. If you work on the culture, walk your talk by showing that coaching is for everyone, and are creative about ways to encourage people to engage, you will find that you're busy with deep and impactful coaching all year long.

Next Steps

What strategies will you use to engage a variety of teachers as you get ready for deeper coaching?

_____

_____

_____

_____

_____

_____

_____

_____

_____

_____

_____

_____

_____

_____

_____

_____

_____

_____

_____

_____

_____

_____

_____

_____

Tools and Artifacts

BLOG

Who Goes First?

BLOG

Moving From an "Opt-in" to
an "All-in" Coaching Model

VIDEO

The Power of
Authentic Engagement

www.dianesweeney.com/launching-tools

Section III

Message and Market Coaching

Move

8

Plan How You Will Message and Market Coaching

Developing the right message around coaching often determines coaching's impact on learning. Some teachers may associate coaching with evaluation or they may have the impression that coaching is about identifying what they are doing wrong. Being thoughtful about how we message and market coaching sets us up to authentically engage all teachers, rather than just a few.

Designing the campaign we use to message and market our coaching work is a move for all coaches, no matter how established you might be in a school. Even if coaching feels like a well-oiled machine, it's still important for you to take the time to create a new plan to message and market your work each year.

Reflect

What message does your staff need to fully understand the coaching role?

_____

_____

_____

_____

_____

_____

_____

_____

_____

_____

_____

What This Move Looks Like

Reaching our audience is always easier when we authentically demonstrate our personality and style. Allow both to shine through as you communicate your beliefs about coaching and the different ways you can engage with teachers to support student learning. Following are some things to consider as you develop your plan.

1. **Start With the *Why***

   With all the decisions teachers have to make at the beginning of the school year, it's natural that topics like coaching fall to the back burner. With this hectic beginning, many teachers forget that the goal of working with a coach is to focus on students and their learning. Getting clear on our *why* for coaching helps us communicate that we are here to focus on students, not to change or evaluate the teaching practice.

   We recommend discussing your beliefs around coaching with your administrator to craft or refine your *why*. This will ensure that you share similar beliefs and are aligned when it comes to your thinking about coaching. When you communicate why coaching matters, teachers can more readily embrace what coaching is and how it will be implemented in your school. To help you establish your own beliefs, here are a few of ours:

- Increased student achievement—for all students, every day—is why we are here.

- It's not our job to fix teachers or be the expert on all things.

- Everyone brings varied experiences and expertise to the table— let's listen to them.

- The goals of others drive our partnership. We aren't here to tell people what to care about.

2. Create a Launching Artifact

Discussing coaching with teachers is an effective way to communicate your passion for learning and your desire to partner with them. Words alone, however, can quickly be forgotten when teachers get back to the job of teaching. Creating a launching artifact is a tangible way to help your message about coaching linger after the initial presentation. Think of your artifact as a tool to communicate all the things you want teachers to remember when you are out of sight.

Artifacts can come in the form of slide shows, animated videos, digital newsletters, and succinct infographics. When planning for your launching artifact, work with your principal to discuss the best ways to communicate with the staff. Keep in mind that the personality of a faculty is unique, and we want to tailor the artifact to match. Teachers will be most responsive to our invitations when they feel they know the real you. While we provide some examples of artifacts in the Tools and Artifacts section, we always recommend making your own.

3. Articulate What Coaching Is and Isn't

Previous experience with coaching can be hard to shed. Because of this, we want to consistently communicate what coaching is and isn't. This is especially critical if you are shifting from a teacher-centered coaching model to a student-centered approach. For example, you might lead teachers through a sorting activity using the stems from the following figure. This will allow teachers to dive deeply into existing concerns and questions so we are not working against misperceptions about coaching all year long.

What Coaching Is and Isn't

COACHING IS	COACHING ISN'T
A partnership	Evaluative
Focused on student learning	Focused on making teachers do things
Good for our students	About fixing teachers
Outcome- and standards-based	A waste of time
Driven by teachers' goals	Driven by the administrator, coach, or district
Flexible and responsive	Fixed and inflexible
Fun and interesting	Something to avoid

Source: Sweeney and Mausbach (2018).

4. Share Multiple Times in Multiple Ways

Starting on the first day of school, teachers will be working at a breakneck pace. For this reason, our messaging and marketing approach must trickle out information slowly and steadily so it is embraced in the moments when coaching is most needed. As we explain in *The Essential Guide for Student-Centered Coaching* (Sweeney & Harris, 2020), advertisers use a process referred to as the "rule of seven." This means that a potential customer needs to hear your message seven times before they buy something from you. Creating multiple ways to "advertise" our work with teachers allows us to be strategic with our timing of sharing a balance of information, celebration, and invitation.

Use full staff conversations at the beginning of the year as your inaugural opportunity, or first pass, to market and message coaching to the masses. We recommend kicking off this presentation with a supportive introduction or co-delivered message from the principal and coach, and including your launching artifact as a useful takeaway for teachers to revisit later. If teachers have participated in coaching in the past, this is also a great opportunity to ask them to share their experiences.

For the next pass, spend time with smaller groups of teachers, such as in PLCs or in grade-level or department settings. Share specific ways you can partner with each group based on their content area and beginning-of-year student evidence. As the school year unfolds, find unique ways to engage teachers in deeper conversations about coaching. This routine contributes to relationship building and provides an audience for sharing more success stories about coaching. Remember the adage "out of sight, out of mind"—coaches never want teachers to forget that coaching support is just a few steps away or think that coaches are too busy to partner around learning.

How to Partner With the Principal on This Move

Developing a plan for communicating why coaching matters and what it will look like requires conversations with the principal. The result will be a clear message that the coach's role is to support teachers to reach their goals for student learning. Use the following questions to guide your discussion:

▶ What is our *why* for coaching?

▶ How might we tailor the message so that we get the best response from staff?

▶ What opportunities can we create for the staff to discuss coaching and their questions about it?

▶ How can we layer our marketing approach to help coaching remain at the forefront of everyone's mind?

Moving Forward

No matter what approach you decide to take with your staff, create opportunities to discuss and explore coaching in ways that will be meaningful. Knowing how busy educators are, we don't want to create more meetings and ask them to read, watch, or listen to things that aren't purposeful. Creating a plan for the entire year will allow you to be strategic with what is shared and when, and having the road map designed in the beginning will save you time as your work builds throughout the year.

Next Steps

How will you message and market coaching this year?

_____

_____

_____

_____

_____

_____

_____

_____

_____

_____

_____

_____

_____

_____

_____

_____

_____

_____

_____

_____

_____

_____

_____

_____

Tools and Artifacts

TOOL

Steps for Building
Excitement Around
Coaching

VIDEO

Principal Sharing
What Coaching Is
and Isn't

SAMPLE

Launching
Artifacts

www.dianesweeney.com/launching-tools

Move 9

Work With the Principal to Advocate for Coaching

The principal is your most powerful advocate for coaching. Coaches who report being frustrated by the lack of participation in coaching often describe a situation where they don't feel like their principal understands how to support the effort. This move will help you steer clear of this frustration by partnering with your principal to envision what this support would look like.

The impact of our coaching thrives when we have a principal who, when talking with teachers, takes advantage of opportunities to encourage coaching partnerships. We can't assume that principals will see these openings or know how to respond when they happen, so starting a dialogue about how they can best do both will help the ongoing promotion of coaching and allow you to feel their active support of your work.

> ## Reflect
>
> How comfortable are you asking the principal to advocate for coaching?
>
> _____
>
> _____
>
> _____
>
> _____
>
> _____
>
> _____
>
> _____
>
> _____
>
> _____
>
> _____

What This Move Looks Like

Student-Centered Coaching is designed to include the entire school community. Determining how the principal advocates for this inclusion goes beyond finding ways to get teachers engaged. When done well, this move provides coaches with a natural avenue to connect with teachers throughout the year. Following are some ways to get the conversation with your principal started.

1. **Build a Shared Understanding of Coaching**

   Creating a shared understanding of coaching gets to the next layer of the relationship with your school leader. Even if your principal has worked as a coach in the past, we cannot assume that their experience prepared them for supporting and advocating for Student-Centered Coaching. We want to be sure they understand that our coaching approach is not a facet of teacher supervision or evaluation. This includes coaches engaging in walk-throughs, observations, correcting undesired teaching practices, or addressing noncompliance issues with curriculum or instructional programs (for more on this, see the Tools and Artifacts section, which includes a video that focuses on practices to avoid as an instructional coach).

Instead, we can leverage the coach as a thinking partner around issues such as analyzing student evidence, building unit and lesson plans, and working side by side with teachers in classrooms as the learning is occurring. This approach builds on the strengths of teachers and considers their goals for growth. These are the partnerships that will have the greatest impact on student learning and building teacher capacity. The following figure from *The Essential Guide for Student-Centered Coaching* (Sweeney & Harris, 2020) provides questions to better articulate the purpose and process of coaching.

Questions for Building a Shared Understanding of Coaching

- Do teachers understand why having a coach is important? If not, how can we better articulate the value of coaching?

- Do teachers understand the beliefs and practices of the coaching model? If not, how can we help teachers to better understand what participation will look like?

- Do teachers understand how coaching will impact student learning? If not, how can we articulate this connection?

- Has the school leader solicited feedback from a broad array of teachers about coaching? If not, how can we reach out and get more teacher input?

- Has the school leader listened to teachers and adapted the plan to address any concerns they might have about coaching? If not, how can we adapt to their concerns?

- Has the school leader communicated how these concerns were taken into account in order to create the plan? If not, how can we share our process in constructing the coaching model?

Source: Sweeney and Harris (2020).

2. Gather Teacher Voices Around Coaching

The best way we can meet the needs of students is by approaching teachers with a high level of respect. One way we can accomplish this is by directly asking teachers for feedback to make our coaching program even better. We can solicit this information through surveys and conversations with smaller groups of teachers or leadership teams. What we are hoping to discover is how teachers view partnering with the coach and what might cause them to be reluctant to work with us. Reviewing this feedback with your principal will shed light on how both of you can further advocate for coaching.

3. **Ensure the Principal Continuously Advocates for Coaching**

   How your principal advocates for coaching is a nuanced skill that requires an understanding of Student-Centered Coaching and the practices that embody our approach. Just telling a teacher to "Talk to the coach" or "Go get coaching" is not what we're looking for. The following figure from *Leading Student-Centered Coaching* (Sweeney & Mausbach, 2018) provides language your principal can use to advocate for authentic engagement in coaching.

Language for Setting Expectations for Participation in Coaching

IF I HEAR . . .	THEN I CAN SAY . . .
"Why would I need a coach? I've been teaching here since the school opened."	"I appreciate your commitment to our school. Now that we are taking a student-centered approach to coaching, we view coaching as being a great resource for all teachers. For example, you might work with your coach when you are about to start a unit that has challenged your students in the past, or you might want to work with your coach on the new science standards. We are all learning how to tap into this important resource, and we all have students with diverse needs."
"Does this mean that the coach is going to report what I'm doing in my classroom?"	"My hope is that coaching isn't something that lives in the shadows. I believe that since coaching is student centered, you'll have a lot of student growth to celebrate. These are important conversations to have."
"Isn't the coach for the new teachers?"	"Coaching is for everyone in our school—new, veteran, all subjects. We all have students with needs, and your coaches are in a great position to help you get there."

Source: Sweeney and Mausbach (2018).

In order to avoid having to hustle for coaching work, we recommend partnering with the principal to establish the paths for teachers to participate in coaching. In addition to what was discussed earlier, consider asking the principal to engage in conversations using the following prompts:

- If you haven't had a chance to engage in a coaching cycle, please consider doing so now.

- You've experienced some great success. What's next for you?

- What learning goals are important to you and your students? Your coaching goal is up to you and should be meaningful.

- Look for information on the launch of a new round of coaching cycles and consider following up to get on the coach's schedule.

4. **Create Regular Celebrations Around Coaching**

Celebrating the success of coaching is a subtle yet powerful way to promote coaching and build momentum. As you meet with the principal at the beginning of the year, be sure to brainstorm how you both can highlight the engagement and success coaching will have throughout the year. Consider times when your staff will be together and invite teachers to share their experiences of their partnership with you. Think about the ways you can celebrate coaching within smaller groups of teachers and dig into the impact your work had on students.

Take advantage of all the ways you can communicate coaching success among the staff. Dedicate a corner of a newsletter, the principal's or yours, to coaching accomplishments. If there isn't a culture of reading emails, you can post copies throughout the school where teachers often gather, such as in the workroom, lounge, and restrooms. It might seem silly to think of these spots, but don't discount the few moments where teachers are a captive audience and will take a few minutes to read something interesting and powerful.

How to Partner With the Principal on This Move

We're sure it's no surprise that your principal's inclusion in this move will drive its success. However, we want to be sure that their involvement goes beyond the planning stages. Here are a few things to discuss while considering their advocacy throughout the school year:

> ▶ Are there conversations the principal has with teachers where coaching could be promoted as an avenue of support?

> ▶ What are some possible ways the principal can authentically advocate for coaching in these conversations?

> ▶ How can we share messages about coaching support and success authentically in large and small groups as well as with individual teachers?

> ▶ When are the best times to check in throughout the year to discuss the ways coaching is supported?

Moving Forward

We know that principals are eager to promote the coaching effort in their schools. Spending time gaining clarity on the steps above anchors support that will pay off in ways that are difficult to achieve on your own. Making time to co-create the principal's advocacy plan allows you to move from soliciting teacher partnerships to focusing your energy on engaging in powerful conversations around student learning.

Next Steps

How will you engage your principal in conversations around advocating for your coaching?

_____

_____

_____

_____

_____

_____

_____

_____

_____

_____

_____

_____

_____

_____

_____

_____

_____

_____

_____

_____

_____

_____

_____

Tools and Artifacts

VIDEO

Three Practices
to Avoid as an
Instructional Coach

TOOL

Front Office
Checklist for
Assigning Coverage

TOOL

Checklist for Getting
Coaching Cycles Up
and Running

www.dianesweeney.com/launching-tools

Move
10

Engage Teacher Leaders

One of the ways we can start the year strong is by engaging our teacher leaders in the launching process. Because teacher leaders have a high amount of social capital and drive a culture of continuous learning in our schools, they are not only cheerleaders for coaching but a source of feedback as well. We recommend starting each year by forming a cohort of these colleagues you can solicit insights from throughout the year.

Starting with a cohort of teacher leaders is a great way to build energy around coaching. In the Tools and Artifacts section, you'll be introduced to a principal who formed a cohort consisting of the principal, assistant principal, four part-time instructional coaches, and a leader from each grade-level and special area team. As a team, they met weekly for eight weeks to learn, grow, and establish a plan for implementing Student-Centered Coaching at their school. At the start of the year, the teachers and coaches from the cohort took the lead in introducing Student-Centered Coaching to the rest of the staff. This is a great example of building coaching from the ground up.

Reflect

What role do teacher leaders play in your school?

_____

_____

_____

_____

_____

_____

_____

_____

_____

_____

_____

What This Move Looks Like

Working with teacher leaders propels us to think beyond the beginning of the school year. These partnerships also demonstrate that we value teacher leaders' insights throughout the months to come. Following are a few ways to engage these colleagues.

1. **Identify Your Teacher Leaders**

   The first step is to identify the teacher leaders in your building. Don't feel limited to formally identified roles, such as grade chairs or department leads. Instead, work with your principal to discuss who embraces curiosity and openness and is considered a positive influence among the staff. Don't forget to include teachers who represent non-core areas such as art, music, technology, business, and so on. Following is a list of qualities to look for when creating your cohort.

WHAT MAKES A STRONG TEACHER LEADER?	WHAT ARE QUALITIES TO AVOID IN A TEACHER LEADER?
• Approaches teaching and learning with curiosity, openness, and positive intent	• Engages in thinking that is narrow or closed
• Considers multiple perspectives when discussing learning	• Isn't inclusive or collaborative in their work
• Is highly collaborative in all settings	• Has difficulty seeing beyond own experiences
• Welcomes the challenge of troubleshooting	• Has positional authority without the desired qualities above

2. **Initiate Coaching Cycles With Teacher Leaders**

Now that you have a plan for gathering your teacher leaders, you can begin tapping into this group to build energy around the coaching effort. In addition to asking this cohort to speak about the power of coaching, invite them into the first round of coaching cycles. This communicates the message that coaching is for everyone and dispels the myth that coaching is only for new and struggling teachers. Use these first coaching cycles as word-of-mouth advertising to ignite additional interest in coaching.

3. **Engage Teacher Leaders in Periodic Check-Ins**

As you consider the big picture for the school year, plan how you'll bring this group back together to offer feedback on the coaching program as a whole. These check-ins provide the opportunity to share celebratory results of coaching and discuss how you might refine your coaching practices and approach. Consider using the following stems to focus these conversations:

❱ Are we communicating effectively about Student-Centered Coaching?

❱ What new practices have been embraced as a result of coaching work?

❱ What coaching work is having the greatest impact on student learning?

❱ What obstacles are coming up that we need to focus on?

4. **Create Opportunities for Sharing Coaching Testimonials**

As your work with them builds, encourage teacher leaders to share their coaching stories and successes with others in order to spark interest among the rest of your staff. Consider using newsletters, faculty meetings, and other ways information is shared. This is an organic way to bring visibility to the power of coaching.

We can invite this group to share about their students' growth as well as the impact your partnership had on their practice. Some of the most open, reflective teachers, considered leaders in their field, may shy away from sharing how they continue to grow as learners and teachers. Getting this group of educators to freely share the impact coaching has had on them sends the message that our own growth needs to be recognized and celebrated alongside that of our students.

How to Partner With the Principal on This Move

Most principals are eager to provide the support necessary to increase coaching engagement in their schools. Your principal will be key in helping you identify a group of teacher leaders to collaborate alongside. Following are points to discuss when it comes to engaging teacher leaders:

- Who are the teacher leaders we can tap into for this cohort?

- How can we empower this group to advocate for coaching?

- What is the year-long vision for this group, including when to bring them together throughout the year?

Moving Forward

As you plan for this cohort, consider how to engage teacher leaders in dialogue about the needs around student and teacher learning that they are seeing and hearing. Lead with an authentic learning stance and explain that their feedback will allow you to refine your practice. It is important that they understand why you have brought them together and that you value their input and partnership.

Next Steps

What steps will you take to engage teacher leaders to support your coaching work?

_____

_____

_____

_____

_____

_____

_____

_____

_____

_____

_____

_____

_____

_____

_____

_____

_____

_____

_____

_____

_____

_____

_____

_____

Tools and Artifacts

VIDEO

School Spotlight
of Shades Cahaba
Elementary

VIDEO

School Spotlight
of Norwood
Elementary

BLOG

Spotlight on Success,
Norwood Elementary

www.dianesweeney.com/launching-tools

Move 11

Listen for Openings

Listening for openings is a practice that starts on the first day of school and continues throughout the year. Openings can come in the form of a direct request for support or they may be more subtle, such as a teacher who has changed grade levels expressing concern about a new curriculum. Think of this move as having your antenna turned all the way up so that no signal (or request for coaching) goes unnoticed or unmet.

Since openings often present themselves as problems to be solved, it can be hard to resist the temptation to immediately offer a solution. A far more effective strategy is viewing existing problems as a way to engage in deeper work with teachers. Not only does this allow coaches to make a greater impact, but it honors the relationship by signaling that problems of practice are challenging, multifaceted, and can take time to address.

Reflect

How do you know when someone is ready for coaching?

_____

_____

_____

_____

_____

_____

_____

_____

_____

_____

What This Move Looks Like

If we aren't listening in intentional ways, then we might miss an opportunity to further teacher and student learning through coaching. The following strategies allow us to become more aware of and responsive to openings for coaching.

1. **Join as Many Conversations as Possible**

   If a coach simply waits for teachers to come to them, they will most assuredly miss openings. Being in all sorts of conversations with teachers creates the opportunity to hear things like "I've never taught this curriculum before," "I've heard that this cohort of students will be challenging," or "I'm excited to try some new things this year." All of these are openings for coaching, and all of these would be missed if you weren't actively engaged in the conversations.

2. **When You Hear an Opening, Act Immediately**

   Acting on openings can include acknowledging that you heard the concern and setting up a time to follow up with the teacher, or making a mental note that this is something you've heard and will continue to monitor. All of these options include different levels of interaction with the teacher, and the path a coach takes will depend on the relationship that already exists. For example, with one teacher it might be quite natural to respond, "Let's work together on that." Yet with another, you may feel the need to nurture the relationship before suggesting a coaching partnership. Tailoring your actions in this way allows the partnership to build organically.

3. **Use Reflective Dialogue to Better Understand Openings**

As soon as an opening presents itself, an opportunity arises for a coach to engage in reflective dialogue to better understand where the teacher is coming from. This provides clarity about what the teacher is thinking, how the students are performing, what has happened already, and what the teacher is hoping to accomplish next.

We know that context matters, and we never want to make too many assumptions about what we are hearing from a teacher. So instead, we listen and gather information through a process of authentic questioning. Whenever you encounter a need from a teacher (any need), a good rule to follow is to ask a few clarifying questions so you understand the whole picture. We provide a few scenarios in the Tools and Artifacts section to illustrate what this feels like.

Self-Assessing Your Behaviors at the Conversational Level

1. What kinds of questions do I ask? Clarifying, probing, other?

2. What nonverbal cues do I send that I'm listening? How do I take notes at the same time?

3. How did I feel during silence or "think time"?

4. How many suggestions did I make? And how much did I build on the ideas of others?

Source: Sweeney and Harris (2020).

How to Partner With the Principal on This Move

Principals can encourage and listen for openings right alongside the coach. Since we advocate for an all-in approach to coaching, this means that any and all teachers are candidates for Student-Centered Coaching. Communication between the principal and coach about the openings that they are hearing from teachers contributes to creating a culture for coaching throughout the school. Here are some questions for the principal and coach to discuss to make this happen:

> What are some settings where we will listen for openings?

> Are there any specific teachers or teams we'd like to connect with so we can build bridges toward coaching?

> How will we keep track of and share the openings that we both encounter?

> Are there any needs that were identified at the end of last year that could be revisited as we return to school?

> How can we use student evidence or data to foster conversations that create openings?

Moving Forward

Listening for openings is an active process that includes both the principal and the coach. When you tune your ear and listen, you'll be amazed by what you hear. Openings are literally everywhere, and each one presents the opportunity to engage in reflective dialogue, build relationships, and kick-start coaching.

Next Steps

How will you listen for openings early in the school year?

_____

_____

_____

_____

_____

_____

_____

_____

_____

_____

_____

_____

_____

_____

_____

_____

_____

_____

_____

_____

_____

_____

_____

_____

Tools and Artifacts

TOOL

Scenarios for Asking
Clarifying Questions

VIDEO

Ways to Respond
to Openings

TOOL

If/Then Chart for
Leveraging Openings

www.dianesweeney.com/launching-tools

Section IV

Get Ready for More Formal Coaching

Move

12

Invite Teachers Into Coaching Cycles

· ·

If you've been reading this guidebook from beginning to end, you're likely at the point where some excitement is building. We feel your energy and are ready to support you in getting prepared to shift your schedule toward launching your first round of coaching cycles.

As we explore ways we can invite teachers into this process, let's remember that coaching cycles are critical because they allow us to work side by side with teachers and their students in a deep and sustained way. If you are a returning coach, it's possible that you have already started cycles with a few teachers. If that isn't your situation, then we will get you moving in the right direction.

Reflect

What excites you about extending an invitation to teachers to participate in a coaching cycle?

_____

_____

_____

_____

_____

_____

_____

_____

_____

_____

What This Move Looks Like

The first step begins with getting your schedule cleared for in-depth coaching work. You have likely been engaging in other informal tasks that have been recommended earlier in this guidebook. It's now time to let teachers know that you will be phasing out those tasks that have less impact on student learning in order to take your coaching deeper. Previously, we invited you to think about some big-picture ways you can organize your schedule. Now it's time to get down to the nitty-gritty.

1. **Create an Invitation That Goes Out to Teachers**

   Now that you have blocks of time open for coaching cycles, you can send out an invitation that includes a synopsis of the messaging information you have given staff up to this point. Briefly reiterate why coaching matters and how your coaching structures are designed to provide further support for teaching and learning. It is also powerful to include your beliefs about coaching and the actions you will take to demonstrate those beliefs in your day-to-day work. The design of your invitation is up to you, but we have found that keeping this communication simple yields the best results. Here are a few things you can ask:

- What goals are you hoping to achieve from our coaching partnership?

- Is there a particular coaching structure you are most interested in? (We'll provide more ideas on this in our next move.)

- What is the content area or course our work will focus on?

- When would you like to co-plan? (We will need a minimum of 30 to 45 minutes each week.)

- What is an ideal time for co-teaching? (We will need one to three times per week.)

- Is there anything you are feeling uncertain about related to our coaching partnership?

2. **Analyze Interest and Build a Schedule**

If teachers are slow in responding to this invitation, don't panic. Remember how many emails they are fielding and how busy they are at the beginning of the year. You can always send out a reminder or give a gentle nudge when you are having conversations in PLCs and team meetings. When responses start coming in, sort the requests based on teacher readiness, student need, and your availability.

We are often asked how many coaching cycles to aim for at any given time. Since more than one teacher may participate in a coaching cycle, we recommend thinking more about the number of teachers rather than the number of cycles. As the year progresses, many coaches find that they can manage to work with between four and six teachers at a time across their coaching cycles. Of course, we should keep in mind that all situations are different, but this is a good goal to work toward.

Checklist: Steps for Creating a Schedule

☐ Decide when you will launch your first round of coaching cycles. When possible, align the start date with when teachers will be kicking off new units.

☐ Create an invitation that welcomes teachers into coaching cycles. If necessary, send reminders.

☐ Sort the responses based on factors such as teacher readiness, student need, and coach availability.

☐ Determine when you will co-plan and co-teach with the teacher. We recommend co-planning at least once a week and co-teaching one to three times per week.

☐ Block out time for your weekly meeting with the principal, coaching team meetings, and any other recurring obligations you might have.

☐ Build your schedule and share it with the full faculty in order to reinforce the coaching role.

Creating our coaching schedule can be a tricky task for even the veteran coach. The key is to build a schedule that you can manage, as trying to fit in more than you can handle will not turn out well for you or the teachers. Remember that you can always add more coaching work to the schedule, but turning your back on scheduled commitments will not serve teachers and will likely undermine engagement down the road. For more on coaching cycles, check out Chapter 2 in *The Essential Guide for Student-Centered Coaching* (Sweeney & Harris, 2020).

3. Advertise Your Schedule

Take a deep breath, because the hard work of creating the schedule for the first round of cycles is complete. As we mentioned earlier, it's important to make this schedule public so that the staff can see how and where you will be investing your time. Publicizing your schedule also allows all teachers to see that your coaching work spans all grades, content, and experience levels of teachers—again, a demonstration of living your belief that coaching is for everyone.

4. Introduce Yourself to the Students

We are so excited that your first round of coaching cycles is ready to begin. Now that you have an organized schedule and the teachers are eager to dig in and get started, you may find that it's helpful to get into the classrooms where you'll be working so you can introduce yourself to the students. This is also a good time to get a sense of the climate and culture within the classroom. We include a video in the Tools and Artifacts section to give you an idea of what this might look like.

How to Partner With the Principal on This Move

Since your principal has more of a behind-the-scenes role in this move, it will be helpful to ask for their assistance in deciding what to phase out to create more time for coaching cycles. For example, setting up classrooms, providing coverage, and assisting with testing are all things that can come off the coach's plate at this stage in the year. Instead of a list of questions to consider, the following are a few things you will want to partner on with the principal as you prepare for this deeper work.

> ▶ Share how you've been spending your time during the first few weeks of school and your vision of an effective coaching schedule.

> ▶ Discuss the impact each of these things has on student learning.

> ▶ Discuss a plan for removing items that do not align with the outcomes you both have established for coaching.

> ▶ Ask your principal to promote the method you use to extend your coaching invitation by sending a supportive message to the staff with a positive reminder to send in their responses.

Moving Forward

As you prepare for your first round of coaching cycles, remember that all good things take time to develop. You may be wondering if taking an incremental (or invitational) approach will lead to the change you are looking for. We've learned that rather than thinking about whether coaching is voluntary or mandatory, it's more effective to take the approach of building capacity over time by honoring teachers' choice and agency. Sure, this may take longer to build, but the impact will be greater in the end.

Next Steps

What steps will you take to get teachers engaged in your first round
of coaching cycles?

_____

_____

_____

_____

_____

_____

_____

_____

_____

_____

_____

_____

_____

_____

_____

_____

_____

_____

_____

_____

_____

_____

_____

Tools and Artifacts

TOOL

Steps for
Enrolling Teachers
in Coaching Cycles

TOOL

Language for Partnering
With a Teacher

VIDEO

Coach Introducing
Herself to Students

www.dianesweeney.com/launching-tools

Move

13

Leverage a Variety of Structures to Build Momentum

There are structures beyond coaching cycles that can be helpful as we seek to respond to teachers' needs in a differentiated manner. These include co-planning lessons, unpacking (or co-planning) units, and facilitating mini coaching cycles. As you reflect on these options, keep in mind that it's essential that we anchor in the intended learning, or what the students need to know and be able to do, before moving on to how instruction will be delivered. This ensures that we remain student-centered no matter which structure we are using.

While we can certainly engage in these practices throughout the year, there is a particular power in using them to build momentum around the coaching effort early on. For example, a coach who unpacks a unit with a team may then suggest working together to implement it in the classroom. This would be a coaching cycle.

Reflect

What structures have you used to organize your coaching work?

_____

_____

_____

_____

_____

_____

_____

_____

_____

_____

What This Move Looks Like

Let's take a deeper look at the different structures you might offer teachers. If you'd like to learn more, we have written extensively about each of them in *Student-Centered Coaching From a Distance* (Sweeney & Harris, 2021).

1. **Co-Plan Lessons With Teachers**

   Working with teachers to plan lessons can be a bridge to more substantive coaching. Whenever we are co-planning lessons, our job is to help teachers accomplish the following objectives:

   ▶ Gain clarity on the intended student learning for the lesson.

   ▶ Ensure that all parts of the lesson are aligned with the learning target.

   ▶ Use the appropriate school or district curricular resources and instructional frameworks.

   ▶ Efficiently and effectively use student evidence to design lessons that meet the needs of all students.

When done in a student-centered manner, this move leads to increased clarity and allows a teacher to envision how the students will be engaged and assessed as learners. For more, check out Language for Gaining Clarity in the Tools and Artifacts section.

2. **Co-Plan (or Unpack) Units With Teachers and Teams**

As teachers are working to establish their classroom community at the beginning of the year, grade-level or department teams are starting to think about upcoming units of study that need to be unpacked, planned, or revised. This can be a great time for a coach to forge new partnerships by joining or facilitating the unit-planning process. In doing so, coaches have the opportunity to unpack standards with teams as they work to determine what students must know, understand, and be able to do by the end of a given unit. This leads to assisting teachers to create learning targets and success criteria related to the overarching goal. Finally, coaches can help ensure that all tasks and assessments are aligned to the targets. In *Student-Centered Coaching From a Distance* (Sweeney & Harris, 2021), we explore co-planning units using the following protocol.

Protocol for Co-Planning Units

1. Determine the goal or intended learning for the unit. Just like a coaching cycle goal, this can be framed as "Students will . . ."

2. Unpack the learning intention into a set of learning targets ("I can . . ." statements). These targets will serve as the success criteria.

3. Plan the classwork, texts, and resources that will be needed to address each learning intention.

4. Plan how the learning intentions and/or learning targets will be assessed.

Source: Sweeney and Harris (2021).

As mentioned earlier, after a unit has been planned together, it can feel quite natural to offer to continue the support as the unit is being taught. This is an easy way to build a bridge from unit planning right into coaching cycles.

3. **Start With a Mini Coaching Cycle**

Coaches need to be responsive to what teachers are facing but also understand the urgency around student outcomes. We recommend mini cycles as a structure that allows us to work toward student outcomes in a way that feels less demanding to teachers. A full coaching cycle moves through the rotation of assess-plan-teach several times over four to six weeks, all within the context of the goal and underlying learning targets for the unit. Mini coaching cycles move through this sequence just once or twice, focusing on a single learning target or strategy for classroom management or engaging students. This makes mini coaching cycles shorter, lasting only about one or two weeks. The following figure shows how a mini coaching cycle follows the same process as a full cycle but is smaller in scope. For more on mini coaching cycles, read the blog at the link included in the Tools and Artifacts or review Chapter 2 from *Student-Centered Coaching From a Distance* (Sweeney & Harris, 2021).

Comparing Mini and Full Coaching Cycles

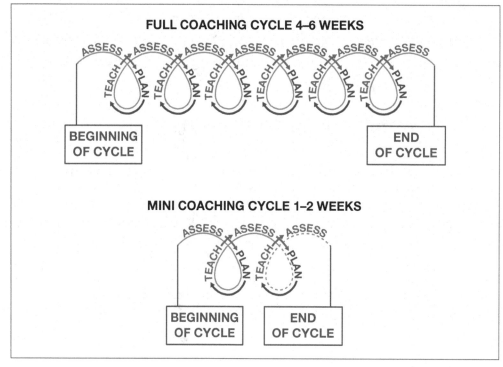

Source: Sweeney and Harris (2021).

How to Partner With the Principal on This Move

As with anything, this effort stands a much greater chance of success if the principal is an active part of the process of making it happen. Here are some questions to guide the principal in advocating for this work:

▶ How can we offer a variety of coaching structures and still stay student centered?

▶ Where are you seeing openings for co-planning lessons with teachers?

▶ How can we create opportunities for teachers to engage collaboratively in unit planning with the coach?

▶ What do you think about encouraging teachers to engage in a mini coaching cycle at some point during the year?

Moving Forward

One thing we learned from the pandemic is that there are several structures in which Student-Centered Coaching can be successful in addition to full coaching cycles. Co-planning lessons, co-planning (or unpacking) units, and engaging in mini cycles are likely to be happening in varying degrees throughout the school year. But there is a particular advantage to partnering with teachers in these structures at the beginning of the school year in order to gain momentum that will continue to engage teachers in the coaching work and ultimately lead to more full coaching cycles down the road.

Next Steps

What strategies will you use to build momentum by using the coaching structures that were introduced?

_____

_____

_____

_____

_____

_____

_____

_____

_____

_____

_____

_____

_____

_____

_____

_____

_____

_____

_____

_____

_____

_____

Tools and Artifacts

BLOG

Leveraging Unit Planning
Into Coaching Cycles

BLOG

Using Mini Cycles to
Take Coaching Deeper

TOOL

Language for
Gaining Clarity

www.dianesweeney.com/launching-tools

Move

14

Plan How You Will Measure Your Impact

··

Coaches often feel anxious about whether they are busy enough, especially at the beginning of the school year. It's easy to see why this would be the case when the coaching role is often undefined. Something we can do right now to harness the start of the year is to plan how we will measure our impact.

In past years, there has been an increased sense of urgency permeating our schools. We simply don't have time to waste in providing students with high-quality learning experiences. As coaches, we also have to operate with this same sense of urgency. That's why we advocate for coaches to develop systems for measuring how their work is impacting student and teacher learning. As a core practice for Student-Centered Coaching, this step is essential and will require some planning.

Reflect

Why is it important to measure our impact?

_____

_____

_____

_____

_____

_____

_____

_____

_____

_____

What This Move Looks Like

This stage in the year is about planning how we'll measure impact over the upcoming months. Here are some ways you can collect evidence of impact as the year progresses.

1. **Plan How You Will Share the Impact of Coaching**

   As coaching cycles are launched, it will be important to measure growth. We recommend using the Results-Based Coaching Tool to collect this information. For more on the Results-Based Coaching Tool, check out Chapter 3 in *The Essential Guide for Student-Centered Coaching* (Sweeney & Harris, 2020) and Chapter 9 in *Student-Centered Coaching: The Moves* (Sweeney & Harris, 2017). We also include a video overview in the Tools and Artifacts section.

   Developing an awareness around your impact creates a feeling of self-efficacy and allows a school to share this information broadly with teachers so that they understand (and value) coaching. As we've mentioned previously, this could include creating videos or other communications with testimonials from teachers about the impact that occurred as a result of the coaching cycle. Graphs that demonstrate student growth can also be posted on school-based social media accounts or shared in newsletters by the principal or coach. As you explore these options, one thing to keep in mind is that no matter how you share the impact of coaching, it is always a celebration of the teacher's effort rather than the coach's.

2. **Continuously Audit Your Time as the Year Progresses**

Regular calendar reviews provide powerful insights into how a coach's time is actually being spent. Coding weekly schedules to report our time usage helps us honestly assess where we are relative to that 60 percent goal for coaching cycles. While it can be tempting to think of this as an effort to count minutes, this isn't the point. Rather, it's about identifying trends related to how you are spending your time so that you can ensure you are making the desired impact on teaching and learning.

This leads to the opportunity to reflect and review your schedule on a monthly, quarterly, or twice-a-year basis. Many coaches examine the data with their principal or with their coaching team, and together they talk about trends, things that are getting in the way, and goals moving forward. Following are some possible categories to consider when tracking how your time is being spent:

- Coaching cycles
- Mini coaching cycles
- Unit planning
- Lesson planning
- PLCs
- Regular meetings at the school or district level
- Personal planning time
- Informal coaching
- Other duties (teaching, recess, intervention, etc.)

3. **Track Engagement Among Teachers**

Another measure that can be tracked across the school year is teacher engagement in coaching cycles. We refer to this as a Status of the Faculty. Setting this up at the beginning of the year provides the opportunity to capture a full year of data, allowing the coach and principal to keep tabs on the engagement from faculty and ensure that teachers don't fall through the cracks. We provided the following example in *The Essential Guide for Student-Centered Coaching* (Sweeney & Harris, 2020).

Status of the Faculty

COACH: ERIC TAYLOR		DATES: AUGUST 19–DECEMBER 17				
TEACHER	RELATIONSHIP BUILDING	DELIVERING PD; LARGE OR SMALL GROUP	PROVIDING RESOURCES	INFORMAL COACHING (e.g., UNIT PLANNING)	COACHING CYCLE
Armisen, Keith (Social Studies)	X	X	X	X	X
Calloway, Sheree (Choir)		X			
Chaney, Melissa (English)	X	X	X		
Guzdar, Dinsh (Social Studies)	X	X	X	X	X
Kreutzer, Rachel (Math)	X	X	X		
Lewis, Veronica (Math)	X	X	X		
Lyons, Marie (Chemistry)		X			

Source: Sweeney and Harris (2020).

4. **Use Teacher Surveys**

Collecting teacher input about the coaching program is also something coaches can plan with the principal. Teacher surveys can be a helpful tool when it comes to measuring the impact of the coaching program as a whole. That's why we recommend considering how to get feedback directly from teachers regarding their experiences with coaching across the year. Included in the Tools and Artifacts section is a survey that can be used to collect information about engagement, student impact, teacher growth, and interest in future coaching opportunities.

How to Partner With the Principal on This Move

Since this coaching move focuses on measuring impact, it's vital for the principal and coach to work together to create a plan. The following questions will guide these conversations:

▶ What are the expectations around using the Results-Based Coaching Tool?

▶ How will we maintain trust and respect when sharing information about coaching?

▶ How often do we want to do time audits across the year?

▶ When and how will we survey teachers so that we have their feedback about coaching?

Moving Forward

It never feels good to be unsure about the impact we are making. But if we don't create a plan, this opportunity may slip out of our grasp. We've seen times when nobody within a system can put their finger on the impact of coaching, and all this does is create stress and uncertainty. Now is the time to start planning for how this important piece will take shape.

Next Steps

How will you work with the principal to create a plan for measuring your impact?

_____

_____

_____

_____

_____

_____

_____

_____

_____

_____

_____

_____

_____

_____

_____

_____

_____

_____

_____

_____

_____

_____

_____

_____

Tools and Artifacts

VIDEO

Measuring
the Impact of
Coaching Cycles

SAMPLE SURVEY

Reflection on
Coaching

PODCAST

Student-Centered
Coaching: The Podcast,
Episode 6, With
Stephanie Anderson
and Kirsten Doebel

www.dianesweeney.com/launching-tools

Move 15

Use Partnership Agreements to Set Norms With Teachers

In *Student-Centered Coaching: The Moves* (Sweeney & Harris, 2017), Diane shared an awkward story about when a teacher who she thought she'd be co-teaching with instead handed her a stack of worksheets and directed her to take a small group of students at a table in the back of the classroom. Many of us have experienced these difficult moments when we were thinking the coaching would look one way and the teacher had an entirely different idea.

To avoid these tricky situations and get our coaching off on the right foot, we must be in agreement about our mutual expectations for the work. This can be accomplished by engaging in partnership agreements and setting norms with teachers. To some, this may feel uncomfortably formal, especially after putting so much effort into building trusting and respectful relationships with them. But if we go into a coaching partnership with the wrong assumptions, we may undermine the very trust we've worked so hard to build. Think of these conversations as less about being rigid and more about being intentional. In this way, we can honor the strong relationships we already have while ensuring that all the right pieces are in place for our coaching to be a success.

Reflect

How will you establish shared norms and expectations with teachers?

_____

_____

_____

_____

_____

_____

_____

_____

_____

_____

What This Move Looks Like

The main thing to think about when using this move is to be clear. Most of these steps involve having a conversation, asking lots of questions, and confirming that you are both in agreement.

1. **Agree to a Schedule**

   We know that our most impactful coaching happens when it's done with consistency over a period of time. That's why full coaching cycles typically last four to six weeks and involve multiple co-planning and co-teaching sessions. In order for this kind of work to happen, it takes more than a laissez-faire "I'll let you know when I want to do this together again" kind of approach from the teacher. Instead, we have to make sure that the teacher understands and agrees to the time commitment involved for the coaching partnership to be successful. This means being explicit, before the cycle begins, about the days and times of the week that you'll be working together. This creates a shared expectation regarding how each of you will engage in the coaching partnership.

2. Set Norms for How You Will Work Together

Whether we had our own classroom just last year or ten years ago, we all remember how much went into building and maintaining our classroom culture. When someone new came in, we might have felt protective or even defensive of this special space. Now, as we think about going into someone else's classroom as a coach, we'll need a strong set of norms in place to be sure that we are honoring and respecting the culture the teacher has created with their students. Here are a few questions to guide the norm-setting conversation:

▶ What rituals, routines, and management strategies should I be aware of?

▶ What do you see my role being with regard to behavior issues?

▶ Are there any students with special needs (language, emotional, developmental) that I should be aware of?

▶ Are you comfortable with us informally building off one another, or do you prefer that we each stick to our own parts of the lesson?

3. Uncover Any Concerns

Even after discussing the questions above, teachers may still be left with some of their own questions or concerns. Again, we don't want to risk making false assumptions, so be sure to offer the opportunity for this to be uncovered. "Do you have any questions that we haven't yet addressed?" is a great place to start. This will provide the chance for a teacher to ask clarifying questions that they may still have about the process and to raise any concerns as well.

For secondary teachers in content-heavy classes, there is often a question about how a coach who doesn't share their expertise could possibly have a role to play in the delivery of instruction. To reframe this concern, it can be helpful to remind the teacher that your role is more about partnering, rather than delivering a lesson, when in the classroom. Another misunderstanding can occur when a teacher's only schema for co-teaching is having the extra adult in the room working with a small group of students. This divide-and-conquer approach undermines coaching because it no longer allows the coach and teacher to practice the following moves that we recommend using when coaching in the classroom.

Options for Coaching in the Classroom

COACHING MOVE	WHAT IT LOOKS LIKE
Noticing and Naming	During the lesson, the teacher and coach focus on how the students are demonstrating their current understanding in relation to the learning targets. As the teacher and coach work with students, they will record student evidence that they will use in their planning conversations.
Thinking Aloud	The teacher and coach share their thinking throughout the delivery of a lesson. By being metacognitive in this way, they will be able to name successes and work through challenges in real time.
Teaching in Tandem	The teacher and coach work together to co-deliver the lesson. The lesson is co-planned to ensure that their roles are clear, the learning targets are defined, and they both understand how the lesson is crafted.
Co-Conferring	The teacher and coach sit side by side when conferring with students. This way, they create a shared understanding of how the students are doing. This then informs the next lesson.
You Pick Four	The teacher identifies approximately four students to whom the coach will pay special attention in order to collect student evidence. The coach keeps the learning targets in mind while collecting student evidence. This evidence is then used in future planning conversations.
Micro Modeling	A *portion* of the lesson is modeled by the coach. The teacher and coach base their decision about what is modeled on the needs that have been identified by the teacher. Micro modeling may occur during a whole group lesson, conference, small group, or so on.

Source: Sweeney and Harris (2016).

Getting on the same page will help get the coaching partnership off to a great start. The following example of a partnership agreement will get you started on having these conversations.

Partnership Agreement for a Coaching Cycle

What Is Our Focus?

- What is our goal for student learning?

- What are the learning targets that capture what we want the students to know and be able to do?

How Will We Work Together?

- There are options for how we can work together in your classroom. Let's talk through these options and pick some that feel right to you.

- There are also options for how we can collect student evidence when we are working together in the classroom. How would you like to go about doing this?

- How will we reflect, both individually and collectively, on our work and students' growth?

How Will We Approach Co-Planning?

- We will need at least 35 to 40 minutes each week for planning. What time works for you?

- It is helpful to create a planning system that works for you. How would you like to share this information (Google Docs, planning template, etc.)?

Source: Sweeney and Harris (2021).

4. Spend Time in the Classroom Before Beginning the Coaching Cycle

Once you've established a schedule and discussed expectations for how you will work together, there's one last piece that will guarantee you'll be ready to get your coaching partnership up and running: ask the teacher if you can spend some time in their classroom. As we mentioned previously, this will allow you to get familiar with their teaching and classroom management style and start to get to know the students. Just remember that this is your only purpose right now. As coaches, we want to be sure that this time in the classroom doesn't feel evaluative in any way, so refrain from taking notes, offering suggestions, or jumping in with students. Simply hang out for a bit, take it all in, and then maybe send a little message to thank the teacher for having you and to tell them how much you're looking forward to working together. This simple gesture will go a long way in showing that you are a true partner and that they are in the driver's seat in this process.

How to Partner With the Principal on This Move

Using agreements and setting norms is something that happens between those who are in the partnership—in this case, the teacher(s) and coach. That said, there are still some questions for a coach to explore with their principal to help with the process:

▶ How can the principal reinforce how important it is for a coach to work alongside teachers in the classroom?

▶ How will we respond to misconceptions about coaching?

▶ In what ways can we help teachers build an understanding of the work and what our shared expectations might be?

Moving Forward

For coaches, trusting relationships with teachers are the bedrock of our work. When we are ready to start moving into deeper coaching with teachers, we want to keep these strong relationships intact and continue to nurture them as we go. One way we do this is by making sure our understanding and expectations for the partnership are aligned between us and the teachers we work with. This gets us off on the right foot from the start and opens the door for coaching that has a big impact on both teacher and student learning.

Next Steps

How will you use partnership agreements and set norms with teachers as you get ready for more formal coaching?

_____

_____

_____

_____

_____

_____

_____

_____

_____

_____

_____

_____

_____

_____

_____

_____

_____

_____

_____

_____

_____

_____

_____

_____

_____

Tools and Artifacts

TOOL

Language for Getting
Ready for Coaching
in the Classroom

VIDEO

Getting Ready for
Coaching Cycles With a
Sixth-Grade Team

TOOL

Partnership
Agreement for a
Coaching Cycle

www.dianesweeney.com/launching-tools

In Closing

By now, the first few weeks of the school year are probably well underway. Teachers and students are settling into the rhythms and routines of their classrooms, and you are ready to reap all the benefits of the seeds you have sown. As you've implemented the various moves we've shared, you have built strong relationships with teachers, forged a thoughtful partnership with your administrator, made a plan to message and market coaching, and laid the groundwork to move into deeper coaching work, including full and mini coaching cycles. You should feel proud of all you've accomplished thus far.

We also hope that the legwork you've done over these past few weeks to set yourself up for success has reminded you of some lessons that are as true for us as coaches as they are for teachers. The first is the power of having a plan. Just like when we ask teachers what their students need to know and be able to do by the end of a unit, and then plan backward from there, we can also see that when we take intentional steps to get off to a strong start with our coaching, the impact we have on teacher and student learning can reach its maximum potential.

The second thing to remember is that the connections we build with others matter. As teachers have spent this time getting to know their students to build a strong classroom community, so too have you been working to gain the trust and respect of your colleagues. These relationships are the bedrock of your work as a coach.

Finally, we are reminded of the *why* that unites us as educators—that it's all about the students. The ultimate goal of our coaching efforts is not to change teacher behavior as an end in and of itself, but rather as a means to ensure that each and every student receives the best education possible every single day. Student learning is the foundation of our partnerships with teachers.

You've cleaned the flower beds, you've tilled the soil, and you've planted the seeds. Now it's time to nurture your flowers and watch them grow!

References

Sweeney, D., & Harris, L. S. (2016). *Student-centered coaching: The moves.* Corwin.

Sweeney, D., & Harris, L. S. (2020). *The essential guide for student-centered coaching: What every K–12 coach and school leader needs to know.* Corwin.

Sweeney, D., & Harris, L. S. (2021). *Student-centered coaching from a distance: Coaching moves for virtual, hybrid, and in-person classrooms.* Corwin.

Sweeney, D., & Mausbach, A. (2018). *Leading student-centered coaching: Building principal and coach partnerships.* Corwin.

CORWIN

A SAGE Publishing Company

CORWIN HAS ONE MISSION: to enhance education through intentional professional learning.

We build long-term relationships with our authors, educators, clients, and associations who partner with us to develop and continuously improve the best evidence-based practices that establish and support lifelong learning.

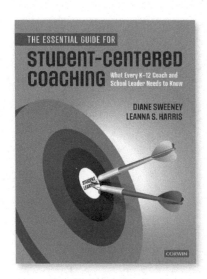
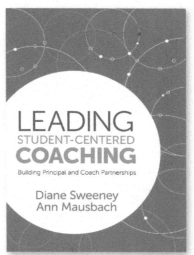
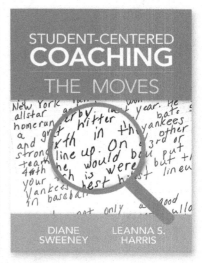